Soccer Tips

Soccer Tips

by
**DAVID
CLEMENTS**

*Foreword by
Professor Julio Mazzei*

Photographs by Gary Nichamin

Julian Messner

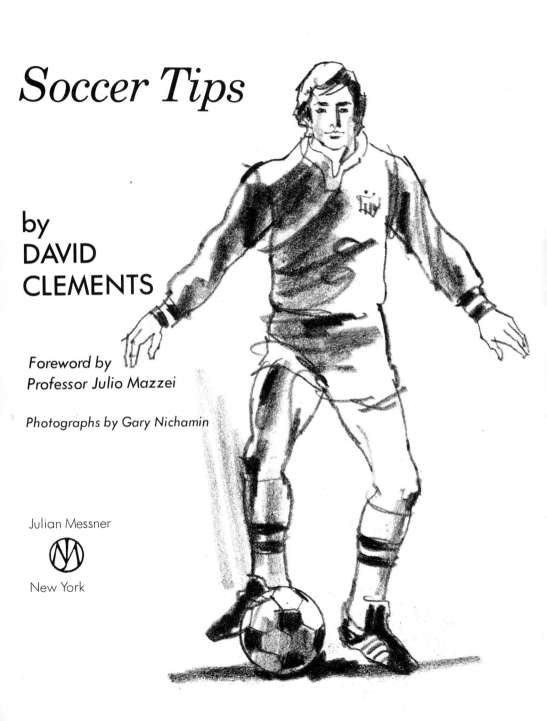

New York

Library of Congress Cataloging in Publication Data

Clements, David.   *Aug. 12/28/78.*
   Soccer tips
   SUMMARY: A soccer guide for the upper elementary grades.
Includes tips on ball control, passing, shooting, volleying, heading,
dribbling, and goal keeping, plus a glossary and game rules.
   1. Soccer—Juvenile literature. [1. Soccer]
I. Title.
GV943.25.C57   796.33'4   77-25009
ISBN 0-671-32956-1

CONTENTS

FOREWORD

On February 23, 1972, in Sheffield, England, the Santos Football Club of Brazil played an exhibition game with the local team, the Sheffield Wednesday. That evening there was a banquet to honor the players of both clubs, and it was there that I met Dave Clements for the first time.

Four years later we met again and, incredibly, we were both working for the same organization—the Cosmos! Dave was a player and I, an Assistant Coach. Two people—one from Northern Ireland and the other from Brazil—renewed their friendship after a practice session at the campus of Hofstra University on Long Island.

On the way to the lockers, that cold February morning, we discussed, among other things, the practice session and the various methods of training.

With that conversation during the 300-yard-walk from the field to the locker room, there began a solid friendship based on mutual respect which continued throughout the 1976 and 1977 seasons and which I expect will last as long as we live. I admired Dave not only as a professional player, but as a man of great intelligence.

When I heard about his appointment as Head Coach of the Colorado Caribous, I was happy for him, even though I regretted his leaving New York. I knew that the Caribous had hired the right man to lead their team to success in the future.

Our paths crossed once more. On October 1, 1977 at Giants Stadium in East Rutherford, New Jersey, the day of Pelé's last game, I met Dave again. It was then that he asked me to write an introduction to his book. And I'm grateful for the chance to tell his readers that this book shows the care which Dave has taken to present the basics of soccer in a simple way, so that everyone can understand the game and profit from his advice.

I am certain that this book will be another achievement in Dave's career.

PROFESSOR JULIO MAZZEI
Assistant Coach, Physical Education
The Cosmos

CONTROL OF THE BALL

The basic principles of control and trapping are simple and few:
1. You should get your body as close to the line of flight of the ball as possible. That requires good footwork. If you have to stretch too far, you will upset your balance and risk losing the ball.
2. Concentrate on the direction and speed of the ball, its flight if it's in the air, and anticipate where it is going to land.
3. Decide quickly which part of your body you're going to use for the control and have the point of impact in line with the ball's path, ready and waiting. Your foot or thigh may just have arrived a second before the ball does, but it is ready to carry out the control you want.

The principle that is used at the moment of impact is the same no matter which part of the body you have selected.

When the ball is about to touch the chosen area of the body, that part must be as relaxed as possible. Just a split second before the ball strikes the stopping surface, that surface should be withdrawn sharply backward in the direction the ball was moving. This provides a "cushioning" effect to reduce the speed of the ball so it's under your control ready to continue.

Good control is an essential ingredient of playing soccer well and enjoying it. You decide what the ball does; you are the boss. To be able to do this takes a lot of practice and patience (staying with it): *patience* because while learning we will make many mistakes and feel like quitting and *practice* because it will help us succeed sooner. Professional players, even the great Pelé, continually work at ball control every day so that they retain and improve their ability.

The Parts of the Body Used in Control

In controlling the ball, which part of the body do you use—and when? We will talk about the feet first and work up from the bottom.

Sole Trap

You can trap the ball using the sole of your soccer shoe. If a ball is going to bounce 2 or 3 feet in front of you, your leg is stretched forward and the foot pointed upward. As the ball hits the ground, bring the sole of your foot down, forming a wedge to "trap" the ball between your foot and the ground.

The insert shows the correct way to trap the ball. This young player is practicing.

Practice

Position yourself about 8 feet from a wall. Throw the ball to hit the wall at about head-height and fast enough so that it will rebound to a position just in front of you. As the ball returns, move forward and "trap" the ball between your sole and the ground on the bounce.

11

Inside of the Foot

The inside of the foot is the most frequently used area to control a ground pass or dropping ball. The reason it is used so often is because it's the largest area available on the foot. The golden rule is the bigger the area used, the less chance of making an error.

For this control, as the ball approaches, the foot is raised about 3 inches, the toe turned outward, and the inside of the foot presented to the ball. For a ground pass, on impact, you withdraw the foot in the direction of travel of the ball and "cushion" it to a stop. With a dropping ball, use the same foot position to start with; then judge the bounce of the ball and going forward slightly, "trap" the ball between the inside of your foot and the ground.

Practice

Take up a similar position as in the sole trap. This time, however, throw the ball a little harder and lower so that it will bounce back a little further, level with you. As the ball returns from the wall, turn your body slightly to one side; turn the receiving foot outward. Then going forward make the "trap" with the inside of the foot as the ball bounces. To practice controlling ground passes use your feet to pass the ball against the wall firmly and on the ground. As the ball rebounds, control the ground pass as described. Continue this exercise alternating feet and you will find that you will always be changing the position of your feet and body as you use first one foot and then the other. This helps with footwork and balance, two essential parts of good soccer play. You can make this a progressive exercise by hitting the ball harder and faster against the wall so the control will be more difficult. Take it in stages. When you can deal with a certain speed in both passing and control, by all means make it harder the next time, but build it into a continuous game, alternating left and right. This will improve balance and footwork at the same time.

Instep

The instep (the laced part of your soccer shoe) is used for steeply dropping balls. This is a difficult skill to master because the part of the foot used is relatively small in area. As a result, there is a high rate of error.

To make the control the leg is raised to meet the ball, with the knee slightly bent, then lowered quickly on impact as the ball is "caught" on the instep. At first you will make the control so the ball lands in front of you, but with a lot of practice you should be able to actually catch the ball on the instep and balance it there. That's "super skill," and when you master it, it's worth showing to your friends.

Practice

If you are alone, simply throw the ball in the air, above and in front of you. Position yourself where it is going to drop. Decide which foot you want to use. Raise your instep until it is level with the knee on the standing leg.

As the ball descends onto the instep, "cushion" its fall by quickly pulling your foot downward as you "cup" the ball on your instep. When you are satisfied with your control at a low height, then progress by throwing the ball higher. Aim for good control at each stage before going on to the next one.

Thigh

When the thigh is used in controlling an airborne ball, nature has given us some help. I mentioned the importance of the "cushioning" effect we must use. We have a natural cushion in the thigh muscle itself. Because of this, you will find using your thigh on a dropping ball can become a consistently useful means of control.

Concentrate hard, as always, on the ball's flight. Adjust your position to the dropping point of the ball. Raise your thigh to meet the ball as it comes down. Then quickly withdraw the controlling leg to take the speed out of the ball, and it should again fall at your feet. Once you have discovered your body's personal balance, you may be able to bounce the ball from one thigh to the other repeatedly.

Practice

For practice, throw the ball up in front of you to a height you are satisfied with. When you improve, you can throw even higher. Watch the flight. Adjust your position and carry through with your "cushion" control.

You can also practice by throwing the ball high against a wall. As it rebounds, get in line with its flight and move to where it is dropping to execute your thigh control.

Chest

Your chest provides a broad strong area that is ideally suited to controlling lofted passes or a ball that is too high for your foot or thigh.

As with all control, you should try to get your body in line with the ball. Watch its flight. As it comes close, thrust your chest forward. When the ball makes contact, apply your "cushioning" technique by leaning the top part of your body backwards. With this the ball should drop at your feet in front of you.

Practice

You can use the same two practices you use for the

thigh since both deal with the airborne ball. Except that now of course you intercept the chest ball higher up than the one on the thigh. This means you'll have to throw the ball higher against the wall or move forward more to meet it higher up on its flight.

The chest is often used to control a ball that is too high for your foot or thigh.

PASSING

Now that we've dealt with control, we can take the next step in teamwork; passing the ball to a teammate.

Your main objective when you pass is to have the ball reach your teammate and be as easy as possible for him to control. To do this you must be aware of his position, his movement, and where players of the other team are.

If the receiving player is standing still, the term used is "playing the ball to feet." If the receiver is running, the ball is played to an area a few yards in front of him. This we call "playing the ball into space." Any of the passing methods we will look at can be used to play the ball "to feet" or "into space."

Good passing is essential in good team play. To make a good pass you must compute the distance, speed, direction, and height of your pass in a split second. Remember that you want it to be as easy as possible for your teammate to manage when he gets it. Intelligent passing is a big bonus for your team.

18

What must you do to pass well? Be on your toes. Know where the other players are, those of the opposition as well as your own. Decide quickly which teammate you will pass to and what method of passing you'll use. Concentrate on what needs to be done and do it smoothly.

Kinds of Passes

Inside of the Foot Pass

An inside of the foot pass is most effective up to a distance of 20 yards. Use the wide, flat area of the inside of the foot. The ball is pushed along the ground with a smooth, firm swing of the leg. Either foot can be used of course.

The kicking foot is turned outward, with the inside of the foot facing the ball and raised about 2 inches off the ground so that the foot meets the center of the ball. (The kicking leg swings with a pendulum movement—a free back and forth movement—as it strikes the ball.)

The support leg is positioned alongside the ball but several inches to the side, with the standing foot pointing in the direction the ball is to go.

Practice

Practice for the inside of the foot pass is easy to do. Simply find a wall and you can play the ball against it repeatedly. Do not stop the ball at all, and each rebound increases the strength and speed of your pass. You can judge your own progress. Over a number of weeks you will be able to make stronger and better passes for a

The shading on the insert shows the proper area of the foot for the inside of the foot pass. Practice for this kind of pass is easy.

longer period of time. Remember to use both feet when you practice. Sometimes use only the left foot, for perhaps 20 consecutive passes, then the right. Then, finally, alternate left-right-left-right, and so on.

Outside of the Foot Pass

An outside of the foot pass is used mostly as part of a dribble and travels only 5 to 10 yards. The pass is diffi-

The shading in the insert shows the proper area of the foot for the outside of the foot pass.

cult for the defense to anticipate because the first part of the movement looks like a normal stride in running or dribbling. At the last moment, just before the foot touches the ground, the ball is flicked away to the side to a teammate. The area used is the outside front edge of the foot. It is an ideal method for short passes made on the run: for example, the first part of a wall pass, or give and go movement.

Instep Pass

There are times when it is necessary to pass the ball over longer distances and with more speed than we can achieve with the sides of the foot.

For these longer distances we can use the instep, that is the laced part of your soccer shoe, not the toe alone. Let me stress now that the instep pass, to be made accurately and quickly, needs a lot more skill and practice than a simple side foot pass. The chances of error are greater because the ball travels a lot faster and over a greater distance. Constant practice and patience are required to do this well. Success will come eventually.

If there is no opponent between your teammate and you, a low instep drive will be the quickest way of passing the ball.

For a low instep drive do not approach the ball directly from behind, but slightly off to one side. This allows you to have a better swing with your leg. As you approach, your support foot should be to the side of the ball. Your body should lean slightly forward over the ball. As you swing your leg back and bring it down along the intended line of the pass, concentrate on the ball. Extend your instep; make full contact with the ball at its center

The instep pass is used to pass the ball over longer distances. The diagrams show the instep and the area of the ball to contact. The illustrations show the proper method.

line as hard as you need to. Keep your head down as you follow through fully with your swing.

The two main things to concentrate on are having your body over the ball and making contact dead center on the ball.

Lofted Instep Pass

The lofted instep pass is used over a long distance when there are opponents between you and your target. If you pass the ball over their heads, they cannot intercept. To loft the ball with the instep, we modify some of the principles for keeping it low.

The diagram shows the exact place to strike the ball to loft it as this young player is doing.

The approach run is the same: slightly off the line you want to pass the ball. The support foot is also placed to the side but farther behind the ball. At the moment of impact, the body should be inclined slightly backwards and the ball struck below the center line to propel the ball upwards. The power with which you hit the ball and how good your swing and follow-through are will determine how far your pass will go and how accurate it will be.

Heel Pass

To add some deception to your dribble, you may want to use a heel pass. The time to use it might be when you

have dribbled, with an opponent following, past one of your own players. At that point, you should swing your kicking leg ahead of the ball, bring your foot sharply backwards, striking the ball with your heel. In doing this you reverse the direction of the ball, take your opponent away—and the pass goes to your team.

There is another way to achieve the same result with a slight difference. On the run, cross one leg in front of the other and while in your stride, using the heel of the cross-over foot, play the ball backwards.

This method is more difficult at first than a direct heel pass but when perfected is more deceptive because it takes place as part of a stride.

Practice

When you practice passing, make a point of doing it smoothly and with a certain flow. Not only does it look better, but a nice full swing and follow-through as you pass will improve your accuracy.

For instep passing with two people, choose the distance you want. One player makes the pass and the other takes the opportunity to work on control. Then reverse the procedure. This way both players get to practice passing and control. If there are three or four players, form either a triangle or a square to practice.

A pass to be effective must be accurate. Work on achieving accuracy first, then increase the speed and distance through practice. Good professional players are accurate over 40 to 50 yards. When you are fast and accurate in passing to a standing target, then perfect passing to a moving player. Ask a friend to help you. Remember, you must figure out his speed and the speed of the ball and place the ball in his running path. When you have fully mastered these skills, we will be looking for you in the pros.

Both a regular and a cross-over heel pass can confuse your opponent by reversing the direction of the ball.

SHOOTING

Shooting is merely an extension of passing. You are in fact passing the ball into the net, though to beat a goalkeeper you usually have to do that fairly hard and fast. The hardest and most powerful shots are made with the instep, the hard bony area on top of the foot. This is roughly the area covered by the laces of the soccer shoe. It's the same area we use for the instep drive in the outfield and is the most commonly used method of shooting.

The method we use is the same as the low instep drive because the ball must be kept lower than the crossbar. Concentrate hard on your balance, where you strike the ball, and a good follow-through to be powerful and accurate. Here are some other ways of shooting using variations of the instep drive.

Banana Kick

The banana kick is particularly useful on free-kick situations (see Condensed Rules) when there is a defensive wall to go around. It is a hard shot on goal. Hitting the ball off center makes it spin; subsequently the shot curves in flight like a banana. You can use either the outside or inside front edge of the instep for this kick. The ball is struck to the left or right of the center.

To get the ball to "bend" from left to right, the left side of the ball is kicked, using either the outside of the right instep or the inside of the left instep. For a right to left "bend," strike the right side of the ball with either the inside of the right instep or the outside of the left.

This particular type of kick is very popular with South American players, and Pelé in particular can achieve a

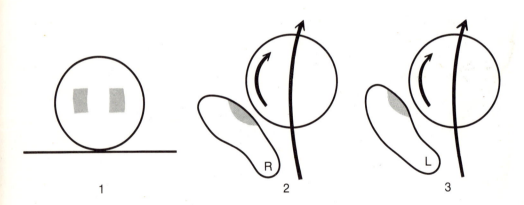

Figure 1 shows the points to contact the ball to make it spin. Figures 2 and 3 show how to make the ball curve right, while figures 4 and 5 show how to make it curve left.

tremendous banana effect, making the ball move several feet off a straight line.

Practice

Practice for these skills can be the same as for instep passing, but do not hit the ball at its center. Contact is made a little to the side and slightly underneath the ball. The leg swing must also exaggerate the banana effect to make the ball have as much spin as possible. This spin causes the ball to bend in flight like a banana.

Remember, shooting must be done at higher speed than passing. Therefore, it must be practiced more sharply.

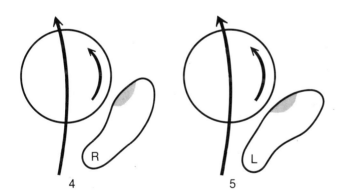

VOLLEYING

Because the ball comes to us from many angles, we need to be able to adapt ourselves to different situations. When the ball is in flight, a volley kick means we don't waste time in controlling the ball and risk losing it. So it speeds up one area of play.

A volley is a kick which is made when the ball is off the ground. The full instep is the surface used to make the kick, and when done correctly, it is the hardest shot in soccer.

A *front* volley is made when the ball is allowed to drop to approximately 12 inches from the ground. With the knee over the ball when contact is made, the action is mostly from the knee.

The *half* volley differs from the full volley in that contact is made just after the ball has bounced and has risen only a few inches off the ground. The same part of the instep is used for the half volley.

Probably the most common volley is the *side* volley. This is taken on either side. The body leans away from the ball at an angle of about 45 to 60 degrees and the kicking leg swings sideways to the ball. Use the same foot area for this kick, although the body angle will be different.

In your shooting, concentrate on having your shots on target, that is, as accurately on the goal with as much power as possible. Remember that with too much power you lose accuracy and the ball may sail high and wide.

The theory is that while the ball is directed anywhere within the area of the goal posts the goalkeeper has to do something positive to make a save and this he may not manage to do. If the shot is high or wide the goal-keeper is safe. So keep the shots on target and make plenty of them.

Practice

Volleying practice is described in the text for each type of kick. It is a different skill, so practice and patience are important if you are to improve at it.

HEADING

Heading the ball is something that is special to soccer. It is just as easy as kicking a ball when you know the correct way to do it.

I recommend you use a light plastic ball or a beach ball to begin practice. When you get your timing and judgment right, then move on to a regular ball, but in each case follow progressive steps. Progression is the secret.

Let's find the proper area of the head to use. Place the palm of one hand on your forehead as if you had a headache. Then adjust your hand so that the top of your eyebrows are level with the lower edge of your hand. Now look up; you should just see the lower edge of your hand. Fine. The area of your forehead in contact with your hand is the correct area to use.

Do not head the ball on the very top of your head because it's a very tender area and you may hurt yourself. The same is true with the back or sides of the head. The forehead is the correct area to use, and it's pretty tough, but treat it with respect. If at any time the ball hurts you, ask someone to watch you to be sure you are doing the right thing. Take the ball in both hands and by bumping it against your forehead in the correct area you will find for yourself how it feels.

This young player has found the correct area of the forehead to use in heading.

Now using the correct area of the forehead, and with your eyes open and your mouth closed, have someone

Don't let the ball hit you. You must hit it at its center.

gently—from one or two feet away—lob the ball onto your forehead. Don't let the ball hit you; *you* must hit it. As the ball approaches, bob your forehead toward it, hitting the ball at its center. Repeat this exercise and build up a rhythm. You will find that after a short time, as the ball approaches, you will have already leaned backwards. Thrust your head and body forward, and head the ball when it comes to you.

Progress a little by increasing the distance to 10 or 12 feet. When you have become good enough to head the ball accurately to your thrower at that distance while standing, then you should work at a jumping headball. Use the same distance, but the thrower must loft the ball enough to make you jump to head it back. Now your timing becomes important, and eventually you should be heading accurately at the maximum height you can jump.

Our final step is when one player 20 to 30 yards away sends you a lofted pass and you can return it to him taking a run and jump, heading the ball at your maximum height. Because this takes a lot of energy, alternate the header frequently. Just to emphasize this point, at professional level we use some heading exercises to keep ourselves fit so we don't get tired too easily.

It is vital that you concentrate and watch the ball all the time. Keep your eyes open so you can see the ball right until the moment of contact. You must hit the ball; it must not hit you.

Remembering these guidelines will help your coordination with jumping and heading.

# DRIBBLING

Dribbling is the technique of running with the ball. Running 20 yards in a straight line is just as much a dribble as weaving in and out of four opponents and gaining 50 yards. We must remember that a pass can travel much quicker than a player dribbling the ball, so in most cases a good pass is best for the team.

If a pass is not possible, a fine dribble can be the best team play and delightful to watch. Dribbling is a great thrill for spectators and should be encouraged at the right time.

Overdribbling, however, is not good for the team; it usually ends with the opponent gaining possession. The perfect combination would be a good dribble, beating an opponent, followed by a successful pass or shot on goal.

The ball is controlled with the inside and outside front edges of both feet. The shading in the diagram shows areas of the foot to use.

Dribbling is closely related to ball control. The areas we use while dribbling are the inside and outside front edges of both feet. Naturally you will find your best foot being used mostly, but it is important to practice and improve your "bad" foot.

Let's start by dribbling a ball between two chosen points 20 to 30 yards apart. On the first run, use your best foot, keeping the ball a stride in front of you all the way, and return. Now do exactly the same with the not-so-good foot; build up your speed but keep control. Now you know the difference in the speed you can dribble using each foot. Now use both feet to cover the same distance, accelerating to your top dribbling speed. This way you can improve your straight-line speed.

Because we can't go straight all the time, we must practice turning, cutting, and maybe reversing direction altogether.

Good balance is important. To achieve it, your body should be inclined slightly forward, with your weight on the balls of your feet. This is the same position you use for running in place.

Dribbling is positive. You must be able to move your body in many directions quickly to keep control of the ball.

Practice

Set six obstacles 5 yards apart in a straight line as markers. If you can get other players, have a competition. Remember, your body balance and close control will determine how fast you can go. Close control is more important than pure speed. Keep within the limit set by your own ability to control the ball. If you go too fast during a game, you lose possession of the ball to the opposition.

Start the practice by zigzagging through the markers and returning, using the areas of the foot we discussed earlier. Do the same thing again, but build up your speed while still keeping control.

Next, go through the exercise using only one foot, but use the inside and outside front edges of it. Then repeat using the other foot.

Work on improving each foot, then both together in all your soccer exercises. Do the same for dribbling as well. Quick turning, short sprinting, and reacting quickly combined with good control are the qualities that make a good dribble possible. These abilities also produce good soccer players. Remember, there is a need for high-quality practice and lots of it.

BALL JUGGLING

Ball juggling is the skill of keeping the ball airborne by playing it with the feet, the thighs, the head, or any part of the body except the hands and arms. It is an ideal practice for controlling the ball.

We must keep in mind juggling itself is only a small part of soccer. But ball juggling as a control practice is great fun, and in competition with friends we can see who is champion at keeping the ball in the air. There are important soccer skills that we develop while practicing ball juggling: (1) the use of our arms to maintain balance and (2) the use of both feet. Use your weak foot frequently to improve it in your juggling. Concentrate on the job to be done and keep your eyes on the ball at all times. I stress concentration because the slightest lapse will result in a dropped ball.

Practice

The laced area of the shoe (the instep), is used but it's the forward part, from the toe to halfway along the laces, that we work with.

Begin, as a first step, by juggling the ball to waist-height. Throw the ball waist-high and let it bounce 2 feet in front of you. After the first bounce, step forward with good balance and concentration, and .kick the ball straight back up in the air again to waist height. Try to keep this going. One kick-one bounce—one kick-one bounce.

Next we keep the ball up for two kicks—one bounce then three kicks, one bounce until we have been able to keep the ball in the air for many touches (contacts).

Now we can try to juggle the ball continuously in the air without the aid of bouncing it.

At first you may only make 2 or 3 touches (contacts) with the ball, but with practice and patience you will become more comfortable doing it. Soon you will increase the number of times you can do it well.

When you want to go a step further, you can vary the height of the ball. This will lead you on to coordinating your feet, head, chest, and so forth. Start with your feet, move up to your thighs, then higher to your head. And finally, chest trap the ball or catch it dead in your instep.

Pelé is an example for all of us. During training sessions he would sometimes start to juggle the ball on both feet only 3 or 4 inches high. After a time he would catch the ball on one instep, hold it there and then flick it over and catch in on the other instep. From there he would start an alternate juggle of varying heights, moving the ball on to his thighs for a time and so on to his head. All the time his concentration and balance were exactly right. As a final show of his skill, he would head the ball in the air and as it dropped, lean forward sharply and catch the ball on the back of his neck. All of this was carried out with such ease and grace that at all times Pelé looked completely comfortable.

Thankfully all of us don't have to have the superb skill and grace of Pelé, but we can try with steady practice to improve our ability as much as possible.

# GOAL KEEPING

The priorities for the goalkeeper's position are
1. To save shots on goal;
2. To intercept cross field passes within his area;
3. To be the first step in a counterattack when he gains possession.

Agility, technique, anticipation, and courage are all needed by a goalkeeper to deal with direct shots on goal. Where possible when fielding a shot, the body should be behind the ball.

The Shots

Here is some advice to help you deal with different shots.

Chest High

For the chest-high shots, your hands clasp around the front of the ball to grasp it securely as it hits the chest.

Ground Level

For the ground-level shot your body is bent and lowered with the foot and knee behind the ball as a back-up for the hands in case a mistake is made.

High Ball

To deal with a high ball face the direction the ball is coming from with your body well balanced. Be prepared to move quickly. Your hands are positioned behind the flight of the ball with the fingers fanned out and the thumbs almost touching. Judge the point where you can safely catch the ball at maximum height, move forward quickly and jump to catch, arms at full stretch.

Diving Catch

For a diving catch your hands are fanned out, as in the high ball. As soon as the ball is caught securèly, the arms are quickly lowered so that the forearm and ball touch the ground first. Keep a firm grasp on the ball and the rest of the body follows.

Deflection Save

If the ball is too far away and moving too fast to hold securely with two hands, you can use one hand to deflect it away from the goal. Judge the ball, make your dive, and with an open hand make glancing contact with the shot to divert it wide. The ball can be deflected to the side or back over the crossbar.

Clearing the Ball

A bonus for any team is a goalkeeper who has good distribution. He may use one of the following tactics to make his play.

Underarm

For players in close range, this is like a side-foot pass.

Low Trajectory (Low Curved Pass)

With teammates a little farther away but with no opposition in between, he can throw a fast, low trajectory pass from shoulder height with an action similar to that of a quarterback.

Lob

To gain distance, with a stiff arm action (like throwing a grenade), he may go for distance and height.

Kicking

The final method of distribution is to punt, drop-kick, or place-kick the ball. In this situation you are going for maximum distance.

# TACKLING

Tackling (taking the ball away from an opponent when you both are using your feet) is just as much a soccer skill as dribbling or shooting. Before I explain technique, I will ask you to treat tackling with respect. If you do it correctly, all should be well.

1. When tackling, make your contact with the ball. Never make contact directly with your opponent first. The ball makes a buffer—a kind of protection—between you and your opponent.

2. Do not attempt tackles when you are too far away. Have your body weight lowered to give maximum balance and compactness. Do not lunge with an outstretched leg because that invites injury to the unsupported limb.

Practice

This practice is for two people, preferably of similar size and weight. In this practice the ball is stationary and acts as the buffer.

The two players should stand on either side of the ball, holding on to each other at the shoulders with outstretched arms. Both players should look at the ball all

the time. Both should use the inside of the same foot to make contact.

Start this exercise gently and build up rhythm and timing.

Muscles in the tackling must be firm and tightly stretched, not loose, to avoid injury on impact.

Both players make contact with the ball at the same time and make it progressively firmer. Making contact at the count of three will soon establish a nice rhythm.

When the rhythm is established, we can then put some more weight into the tackle and concentrate on getting the body weight behind the ball.

 # TEAM PLAY

Soccer is a team game. Good players understand this and are ready to help each other and follow the coach's battle plan. He knows best the many factors which must be considered to decide tactics.

Positions

There is always one *goalkeeper;* he is the only player who may use his hands. He must be flexible and quick— to stop fast, awkward shots from all angles—and be able to kick a long distance and throw accurate passes, long and short.

Fullbacks, sometimes called *outside* or *wing full-backs,* must be fast enough to guard the opposition winger, usually the fastest on a team. To get the ball and start new attacks, fullbacks must tackle and pass well.

Center backs are often tall, since they must head clear a lot of passes. One of the two center backs normally marks, or covers, the opposing center forward, while the other acts as *sweeper*, cleaning up stray passes and unmarked players in his area.

There may be either two or three *midfielders*. Each one is a link between offense and defense. Midfielders are playmakers and must hustle to get the ball to the forwards in a good position to advance or score. Sometimes they score themselves.

Wingers play on the outside and feed the strikers with cross-field passes. Usually small and fast with good footwork, they score some goals, but not as many as *strikers*, who are nearest to the goal. It is fairly common to have twin strikers—a tall, strong main striker (the *center forward*) to head high crosses and a small, nimble player to assist him.

Formations

A 4-3-3 formation has a left- or right-winger up with the forwards.

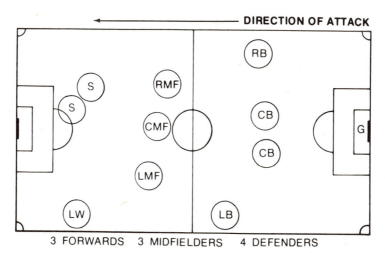

DIRECTION OF ATTACK

3 FORWARDS   3 MIDFIELDERS   4 DEFENDERS

Key: R—Right / C—Center / L—Left / S—Striker
W—Wing / MF—Midfielder / B—Back / G—Goalkeeper

When a 4-2-4 formation is on offense, both wingers are well forward, making four main attackers.

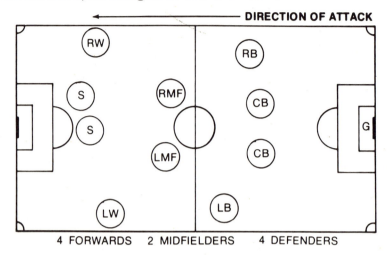

4 FORWARDS   2 MIDFIELDERS   4 DEFENDERS

On defense, in a 4-2-4 formation the two wingers drop back with the midfielders. In effect, the 4-2-4 becomes a 2-4-4.

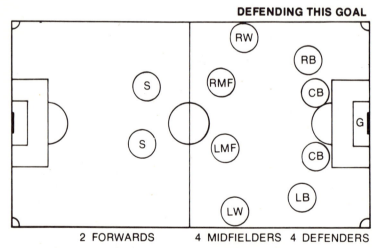

2 FORWARDS   4 MIDFIELDERS 4 DEFENDERS

Key: R--Right / C—Center / L—Left / S—Striker
W—Wing / MF—Midfielder / B—Back / G—Goalkeeper

GLOSSARY OF SOCCER TERMS

Center—to pass the ball from a wide position on the field into the penalty area.

Charge—pushing the opponent off balance legally by shoulder to shoulder contact.

Clear—a throw or kick by the goalkeeper or a kick by the defender in an attempt to get the ball away from the goal area.

Cross—same type of pass as center.

Defender—primarily a defensive player who assists the goalkeeper in protecting the goal.

Dribble—a way of advancing the ball past defenders by a series of short taps with one or both feet.

Forward—primarily an attacking player whose responsibility is to create and score goals.

Goalkeeper—the last line of defense. The only player who can use his hands within the field of play. He is limited to using his hands only within the penalty area.

Half Volley—kicking the ball just as it is rebounding off the ground.

Hands—illegal act of intentionally touching the ball with the hands or arms.

Heading—a method of scoring, passing and controlling the ball by making contact with the head.

Linkman—another name for midfielder.

Lob—A high, soft kick taken on the volley, lifting the ball over the heads of the opponents.

Marking—guarding an opponent.

Midfielder—is both an offensive and defensive player who is primarily responsible for linking the forwards and defenders.

Obstructing—preventing the opponent from going around a player by standing in his path.

Overlap—the attacking play of a defender going down the touchline past his own winger.

Pitch—another name for the field of play.

Save—the goalkeeper stopping an attempted goal by catching or deflecting the ball away from the goal.

Screen—retaining possession and protecting the ball by keeping your body between the ball and opponent.

Sliding Tackle—attempting to take the ball away from the opponent by sliding on the ground.

Striker—a central forward position in the team with a major responsibility for scoring goals.

Sweeper—a defender who roams either in front of or behind the defender line to pick up stray passes.

Tackling—attempting to take the ball away from the opponent when both players are playing the ball with their feet.

Trap—controlling a ball passed close to the player by means of the feet, thighs or chest.

Volley—kicking the ball while it is in flight.

Wall Pass—a pass to a teammate followed by a first time return pass on the other side of the opponent (give and go).

Wing—an area of the field near the touchline.

Winger—name given to the right and left outside forwards.

4-3-3—the player formation most used today (a goalkeeper, four defenders, three midfielders, three forwards).

4-2-4—most used alternative formation to the 4-3-3 (a goalkeeper, four defenders, two midfielders and four forwards).

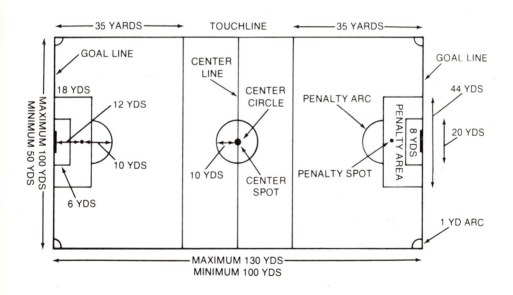

CONDENSED RULES OF SOCCER

Rule 1—The Field of Play. (See diagram on page 61)

Rule 2—The Ball (NASL approved ball—Adidas) circumference 27"-28" (the measurement around the ball), weight 14 oz.-16 oz.

Rule 3—Number of Players. Each team consists of eleven players, one of whom must be the goalkeeper. A maximum of three substitutes may be used.

Rule 4—Player Equipment. Consists of a shirt, shorts, stockings and shoes. Goalkeeper must wear colors which distinguish him from the other players.

Rule 5—Referees. One referee is appointed for each match. He is responsible for control of the game and his decisions are final.

Rule 6—Linesmen. Two linesmen assist the referee by indicating offside when the ball is out of play, and which team is entitled to the corner kick or throw in.

Rule 7—Duration of the Game. Shall be two equal periods of 45 minutes unless otherwise agreed upon.

Rule 8—The Start of Play. A flip of coin decides which team will kick off. Each team must stay on its own half of the field and the defending players must be at least 10 yards from the ball until it is kicked.

After a goal the team scored upon will kick off. After halftime the teams change ends and the kickoff will be taken by the opposite team to that which started the game. A goal cannot be scored directly from a kickoff.

Rule 9—Ball In and Out of Play. The ball is out of play when (a) it has wholly crossed the goal line or touchline, whether on the ground or in the air, or (b) when the game has been stopped by the referee.

Rule 10—Method of Scoring. A goal is scored when the whole of the ball has passed over the goal line, between the goal posts and under the crossbar.

Rule 11—Offside. A player is offside if he is nearer his opponents' goal line than the ball at the moment the ball is played unless, (a) he is in his own half of the field of play, (b) there are two of his opponents nearer to their own goal line than he is, (c) the ball last touched an opponent or was last played by him or (d) he receives the ball direct from a goal kick, a corner kick, a throw in, or when it was dropped by the referee. Note: This is the Traditional Rule. In 1973 the NASL introduced a "Blue Line" Concept with a line drawn the width of the field 35 yards from each goal (see diagram on page 61). Under it, an attacking player is not offside until he is within 35 yards of his opponents' goal rather than midfield, as under the traditional rule.

Rule 12—Fouls and Misconduct. A player who intentionally attempts to or actually: (1) kicks, (2) trips, (3) jumps at, (4) charges violently, (5) charges from behind, (6) strikes, (7) holds or (8) pushes an opponent, or (9) intentionally handles the ball shall be penalized by a direct free kick. Any one of these nine offenses committed in the penalty area by a defender will result in a penalty kick to the offensive team.

A player committing less flagrant violations such as offside, dangerous plays, obstruction or ungentlemanly conduct will be penalized by an indirect free kick.

Rule 13—Free Kicks. Are classified into two categories. "Direct" (from which a goal can be scored directly against the offending side) and "Indirect" (from which a goal cannot be scored unless the ball has been touched by a player other than the kicker before entering the goal).

For all free kicks the offending team must be at least 10 yards from the ball until it is kicked.

Rule 14—Penalty Kick. A direct free kick taken at the penalty mark. All players except the player taking the kick and the goalkeeper must stay outside the penalty area and at least ten yards from the ball (hence the arc at edge of penalty area).

Rule 15—Throw In. When the ball has wholly crossed the touchline it is put back into play by a throw in from the spot where it went out and by a player from the opposite team that last touched it. A goal cannot be scored directly from a throw in.

Rule 16—Goal Kick. When the ball has wholly crossed the goal line after being last touched by a player from the attacking team, it is put back into play by a kick from the goal area by the defending team.

Rule 17—Corner Kick. When the ball has wholly crossed the goal line after being last touched by a player from the defending team, it is put back into play by a kick from the corner on the side the ball went out by the attacking team.